TO:

FROM:

children's answers to everything

Carefully selected by
Richard Harrison and Albert Adler
and illustrated by Hilde Hoffmann

AN ESSANDESS SPECIAL EDITION
New York

CHILDREN'S ANSWERS TO EVERYTHING
SBN 671-10369-5

Copyright, ©, 1969 by Richard Harrison and Albert Adler.
Illustrations copyright, ©, 1969 by Simon & Schuster, Inc.
All rights reserved.
Published by *Essandess Special Editions,*
a division of Simon & Schuster, Inc.,
630 Fifth Avenue, New York, N. Y. 10020.

Printed in the U. S. A.
Second Printing

INTRODUCTION

From the day Junior masters his first "Dada," until he reaches the age of reason, his potential as a natural comedian is inherent in his speech. Every parent remembers "rolling in the aisle" from at least one of his offspring's verbal bombs.

The fireworks included in this book were collected over a period of years and they represent a cross section of humor, from colorful expressions that only a child could create, to the innocent "put down" of the very young.

You may find one of your own youngster's original witticisms between the covers of this book. Don't be concerned unless he has a history of swiping other comic's material. He's probably like the eight-year-old violinist who was out playing ball while his sister still practiced—he finished his half of the duet first.

Directed to remove the gum from her mouth,
young Carol responded with wide-eyed honesty:
"I can't. It fell down my throat."

At seeing a peacock, Patricia blurted out,
"*Look, Ma, one of the chickens is in bloom.*"

While at the zoo, little Billy observed,
*"The lion is standing up in front
and sitting down in back."*

*"My mother can wear every one of her birthday
presents except the electric toaster."*

After frequent falls on her roller skates,
little Carole said with exasperation,
*"I wish I could bend the other way
so I could fall on my lap."*

The father was urging his son to come out
to the deeper water in the swimming pool.
Little Teddy querulously remarked,
"I like to swim where the top is closer to the bottom."

"Do you have to go to heaven
to be a Godmother?"
asked six-year-old Margaret Anne
of her Sunday school teacher.

"*I got a grief case for school,*"
was the joyous proclamation
of five-year-old Billy
upon returning home
from a shopping trip
with his mother.

"Who won the Booby prize?" asked Mother.
"We didn't play Booby," retorted Irene.

"What are you doing for your cold?"
asked Tommy's neighbor.
"I sneeze whenever it wants me to,"
answered Tommy.

*"Porcupines have long needles in them so they
can hurt you when you try to take their pork."*

Returning home late, Susan was ordered
to hurry to bed and not to forget to say her prayers.
Climbing into bed without praying, she whispered,
"No use waking God up at this hour of the night."

Robbie's jaw hurt him when he chewed.
"Chew on the other side,"
commanded Mother.
*"Well, when I chew on one side,
both sides chew,"* grumbled the boy.

Barbara was told to stay indoors
until the heavy rain had stopped.
She looked up at her mother anxiously and asked,
"But, can I go outside when the mud tightens up?"

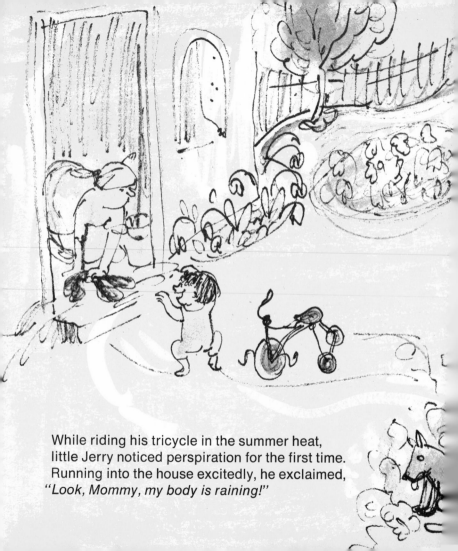

While riding his tricycle in the summer heat,
little Jerry noticed perspiration for the first time.
Running into the house excitedly, he exclaimed,
"Look, Mommy, my body is raining!"

At first discovering his pulsebeat,
Mike remarked, *"I got hiccups in my wrist."*

"*I hurt my toe,*" complained little Joanne.
"Which one?" asked the concerned mother.
"*My youngest one,*" came the reply.

Young Philip threw his loving little arms
around his father's neck
and whispered in confidence,
"Daddy, you know your hair is wearing out."

"Wind is air in a hurry."

At breakfast, little Jackie pouted:
"But I can't eat the scrambled eggs.
You got some egg bone in them."

"I don't like baths—
can't you just dust me off?"

Asked what she liked best about Christmas
after opening her presents,
seven-year-old Maureen answered:
"Standing under the kisseltoe."

"I don't want a tutor—I want a drum."

Asked which animal he thought ate
the least, six-year-old Tommy replied:
"I think it must be the moth.
He eats holes."

"A playwright is someone
who doesn't cheat at games."

"Look, Mother is plastering the cake."

"*In class everybody makes so much noise,
the teacher can't hear me being quiet,*"
was the report Marie Taylor received
from her six-year-old Ginny.

"Synonym,"
explained ten-year-old Buddy
to his friend,
"is the word you use
when you can't spell the other word."

Curious about little Jack's constant
reference to Audrey, Mother asked,
"Who's Audrey?" Impatiently, Jack retorted,
"That's Audrey's mother's little girl."

After getting the report about the fight between
her child and a neighbor's, the mother asked,
"Did you hit her back?"
"*No,*" whimpered the child, "*I slapped her face.*"

Espying the sign:
SHOES SHINED INSIDE—15¢
little Robert questioned,
"Why do people have their shoes shined inside?"

"My foot's asleep. It feels like ginger ale."

"If I waste my manners now,"
said reluctant Ruthie,
"I won't have any left when company comes."

*"Butter makes bread taste bad
when it isn't on it."*

Dad: "When I was your age
I wouldn't think of telling a lie."
Georgie: *"How old were you when you started?"*

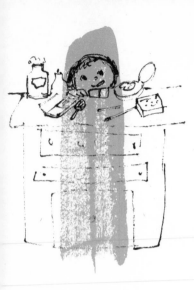

Five-year-old Sally to her mother
who is applying her makeup:
*"Are you going to write on
your eyebrows tonight?"*

*"If you want to get over that fence,
you have to crawl under it."*

"Who beats when you and your brother fight?"
"My mother beats us both."

"My Grandaddy sleeps out loud."

Called upon by his father
to give an account
of his work in English class,
young Ricky stated proudly:
*"We're learning words of
four cylinders now."*

"Jimmy, you're a pig,"
 chastized the father at the dinner table.
"Do you know what a pig is?"
"Yes Sir," said Jimmy.
"It's a hog's little boy."

Comparing notes after a visit to the circus,
eight-year-old Richard remarked with disappointment:
"The knife thrower was terrible.
He missed the girl every time."

After a harrowing experience,
little Margie was asked, "Were you frightened?"
"Yes," she replied,
"and I would have fainted, too, if I knew how."

When asked by his father
if he had cleared the toy-littered floor
of his bedroom, Glenn replied,
"No, but I made a path to the bed."

"I want the nuts with the wood on them."

"Susie," asked her Uncle Al, "do you know
what comes after 'A' in the alphabet?"
Susie pondered for a moment
and then brightened. *"I think
it must be the rest of the letters."*

Child No. 1: *"My father is an Elk."*
Child No. 2: *"How much does it cost to see him?"*

Father to little Marie who was dawdling over her meal:
"When I was your age, I didn't have bread and butter."
Marie's reply: *"You're a lot better off
since you came to live with Mommy and me."*

Seeing brussels sprouts for the first time,
five-year-old Lorin shouted gleefully:
"We got samples of cabbage."

"Our refrigerator grows ice."

"A pony is a little puppy horse."

"Is Mother letting
her hair grow?"
asked Aunt Ida.
*"She isn't letting it;
her hair is doing it
because it wants to,"*
replied Lottie.

*"I was so scared
my heart beat all night!"*

As we emerged from driving
through the long dark tunnel,
Johnnie, age five, quipped,
"*Mother, is it tomorrow already?*"

As she was leaving to do her marketing,
Mother had a last minute request
from four-year-old Patrick:
*"Will you get a pumpkin
and make us an apple pie?"*

Asked if he liked his little sister's
new Easter ensemble,
four-year-old Billy
answered with a question:
"Does it have a hat to rhyme?"

"I can't eat this sauerkraut,"
complained Jeff, age four,
"it's too tangled up."

Wee Barbara visiting her ailing grandmother asked wistfully, *"Will you ask the trained nurse to do some tricks?"*

"Icicles are especially stiff water."

"Jesus' last name is Christ,"
 explained Jeannie
 with all the wisdom of six years,
"and God's last name is Blessus."

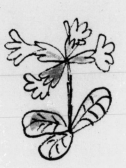

Mother:
"Do you want your orange cut in quarters?
 Age fiver:
"Could I have it in nickels?"

"Please carry me, Dad,"
whimpered Betsy,
"I'm too heavy for my feet."

Describing his ride in an elevator,
little Eddie said,
*"I walked into a little room
and the upstairs came down."*

On hearing the adults talk about a bird dog,
little Margie interrupted with, *"Can he fly?"*

"I can't find the end of this cord,"
shouted the frustrated father.
"Maybe somebody cut it off,"
suggested six-year-old Harry.

"If I sit on the piano stool,"
complained Thelma,
"I can't reach the brakes."

Seven-year-old Sean was trying
to explain to his friend next door
why they were in different schools.
"You see," he said,
*"I have to go to Parochial School
because I'm a Catholic and not a Public."*

"Be a good girl and mind your mother,"
directed the departing father.
"Mother likes to mind herself,"
came the response.

Five-year-old Tommy thoughtfully asked his father
as they drove away from the filling station,
*"How are you going to turn corners, Daddy,
if you put straight gas in the car?"*

New neighbor to child playing in front of her house: "Do you have any brothers?" The child: *"I have only one, and he is me."*

"I want a little tiny diamond ring
for my birthday,"
Maria told her mother.
"Then, we can grow up together."